BROTO

Adèle Wallis

AN OMF BOOK

© OVERSEAS MISSIONARY FELLOWSHIP
(formerly China Inland Mission)

Published by
Overseas Missionary Fellowship (IHQ) Ltd.,
2 Cluny Road, Singapore 1025, Republic of Singapore

First published...........................1987
Reprinted 1990

OMF BOOKS are distributed by
OMF, 404 South Church Street, Robesonia, Pa 19551, USA
OMF, Belmont, The Vine, Sevenoaks, Kent, TN13 3TZ, UK
OMF, P O Box 849, Epping, NSW 2121, Australia
OMF, 1058 Avenue Road, Toronto, Ontario M5N 2C6, Canada
OMF, P O Box 10159 Balmoral, Auckland, New Zealand
OMF, P O Box 41, Kenilworth 7745, South Africa
and other OMF offices.

ISBN 9971-972-61-1

Printed in Singapore
5K/KHL/1990

Contents

Chapter 1

Time to get up

Broto was awake. Morning sounds and smells were all around him. Mother cooking breakfast on a wood fire in the kitchen. The creak of the bucket as it was let down into the well. The sound of splashing as his brother poured the water over himself.

That sound made him get up and go out to the yard. He squatted by the bucket. Scooping up the water with an old coconut shell, he poured it over himself. It took his breath away, but now he was really awake.

Dressing quickly he reached for a handful of rice, and called, "Koor, koor, koor!"

The chickens came running to him. He scattered the rice on the ground. They pecked it eagerly and looked for more.

"No, you can't have more!" he told them. "Rice is too precious! You'll have to go and find your own food now."

Inside the house, Broto's mother had put a bowl of steaming rice on the table. Broto helped himself to rice and vegetables. His brothers were already eating. School started early, and they had to walk a long way. Broto was too small to go to school yet.

"Are you looking after the ducks with Pak Kasim today?" his father asked.

"Yes, he says I'm good at it!" Broto answered.

His father smiled as he picked up the tin bowl of rice which Mother had wrapped in a cloth for his dinner. Putting on his hat, he set off for the rice fields.

Chapter 2

A hundred white ducks

Broto took his lunch from the table and put it in a plastic bag. He liked to go out and take his lunch with him.

Broto's brothers were already waiting for him. "Hurry up, Broto, or we'll be late for school!" they said. Broto's brothers always walked with him part of the way to Pak Kasim's house. Pak Kasim and Ibu Kasim were neighbours.

Broto waved goodbye to his mother and baby Sari. "Take care on the road!" Mother called after him. Broto nodded and ran to catch up. His brothers' legs were longer than his, and he had to walk fast to keep up with them.

There were not many cars on the road yet. A buffalo cart was creaking slowly along.

Soon they reached the path to Pak Kasim's house. Broto said goodbye to his brothers and started up the path through the rice fields. Ah, there was Pak Kasim waiting for him. He looked a little worried today, but he smiled as Broto came up.

"Little Hanna is sick," he explained.

Broto could see Ibu Kasim rocking the baby to and fro in the cloth sling tied over her shoulder. She saw Broto and came out of the house with some bananas

for their dinner. Broto liked Ibu Kasim. She was quiet and had a nice smile.

"You can go and let the ducks out now, Broto," said Pak Kasim.

Broto went to the duckpen and opened the bamboo door. The ducks came waddling out noisily, looking here and there for little-bits of food to eat.

Pak Kasim handed Broto a long bamboo pole with leaves on the end. Broto felt proud as he held the stick. Carefully he dangled the leaves in front of the first duck to lead him on. The other ducks followed, and soon Broto was leading a long line of a hundred white ducks along the road.

Pak Kasim walked behind the ducks, watching them carefully. Pak Kasim took great care of his ducks. He needed the money he got when he sold their big blue eggs.

It seemed a long walk to Broto. At last they passed a wide, muddy river, and came to some rice fields that had just been harvested. Here they left the road and led the ducks into the field. The ducks scattered and began to hunt around for grains of rice that had been left behind.

Chapter 3
Praying for Hanna

Pak Kasim and Broto sat down under a shady tree. Broto stuck the bamboo pole in the ground. No need for that now -the ducks could wander around and find food, while he and Pak Kasim watched to see that they didn't get lost.

Broto looked at Pak Kasim. His eyes were closed. Surely he couldn't be sleeping already? Just then Pak Kasim opened his eyes.

"I thought you were asleep, Pak Kasim!" Broto said.

Pak Kasim smiled. "I wasn't asleep, Broto. I was praying."

"Praying for Hanna?"

Pak Kasim nodded.

Broto was puzzled. "But you can't pray in a field ... and just like that in those clothes ... and anyway, I didn't hear you say anything!"

Broto knew that Pak Kasim was a Christian. Once Broto and his family had gone to a Christmas service in Pak Kasim's church. Since then, Broto and his brothers had started going to Sunday School. But he thought you had to go into a church to pray.

"No, Broto," Pak Kasim said. "You don't have to go to a special place to pray. Christians believe that you can pray to God anywhere and about anything. And God understands all about us, so we can even speak to Him in our hearts, and He hears us."

Broto thought about that. It was all so different. But he liked the Christians he had met. He hoped his father would let him keep going to Sunday School.

The sun was getting hotter. Broto began to feel hungry.

"Pak Kasim, is it dinner time yet?" he asked.

Pak Kasim laughed. "You're always ready to eat, aren't you, Broto? Yes, we'll eat now." He reached for his rice bowl, and Broto unwrapped his.

"Would you like me to pray out loud this time?" Pak Kasim asked. Broto nodded. Then Pak Kasim prayed, "Thank You, Lord, for all Your kindness to us. And thank You for this food You have given us. Bless it to us. Amen."

Broto and Pak Kasim ate their rice. Broto had some dried fish with his vegetables, and Pak Kasim had a hard-boiled duck egg with his. Then they ate the bananas Ibu Kasim had given them.

Chapter 4

Broto is left in charge

Broto was just wrapping up his empty container when he saw someone walking quickly along the road towards them. It was Pak Kasim's oldest girl. She looked as if she'd been running.

"Mummy says she needs to take Hanna to the doctor," she panted. "She'd like you to take her there, Daddy."

Pak Kasim stood still for a minute, looking as if he didn't know what to do. Then he looked at Broto.

"That's all right, Pak Kasim," Broto said. "You go, and I'll look after the ducks!"

Pak Kasim said, "All right, Broto. But don't try to bring them home on the big road. Wait for me here, and I'll come back as soon as I can."

Broto watched Pak Kasim and his daughter walking along the road until he couldn't see them any more. He felt proud that Pak Kasim had left him to look after his precious ducks. Broto counted them, "Ninety eight, ninety nine, a hundred." Yes, they were all there. Some had their heads down, still eating, while others were resting quietly.

Broto looked along the road. It wasn't very busy, as it was the hottest part of the day. Two women were coming along with bundles of newly-harvested rice on their heads. The man behind had big golden tassels of rice hanging from a pole over his shoulder. Bounce, bounce, bounce. The rice tassels bounced as the man trotted along the road. Broto looked back at the ducks walking around, their tails wagging from side to side. Waddle waddle ... bounce bounce ... Broto was getting drowsy.

Chapter 5

In the river

"Hey, wake up, Broto!"

Broto opened his eyes. His friend Amir was grinning at him. He was sitting on the back of a water buffalo.

"I've got to give the buffalo a wash," he said. "Come and have a swim with me!"

"Oh, but I can't Amir. Pak Kasim had to go and take Hanna to the doctor, and he's left me to look after the ducks!"

"The ducks are all right," smiled Amir. "We won't be long. The ducks will still be here when you come back!"

Broto looked at the ducks again. They certainly looked very busy. They wouldn't know he wasn't there. And it *was* hot. A swim would feel so good.

"All right," he said. "But I mustn't be long."

Broto climbed up behind Amir on the buffalo's wide back. The buffalo lumbered slowly off towards the river.

When they got to the river, Broto and Amir slipped down, took off their shirts and jumped into the brown, muddy water.

"Look, your buffalo is so happy to be in the water, he's nearly smiling!" laughed Broto. He and Amir picked bunches of grass from the side of the river and rubbed the buffalo's dusty sides. Then they splashed water on him and rubbed him again. Sometimes the water splashed on them instead, and soon they were having fun throwing water at each other. The buffalo squatted down in the river with only his horns and nose showing above the water.

When Broto and Amir were tired of splashing water, they waded up the river to a place where there were big rocks sticking out of the water. It was fun jumping from rock to rock and trying to catch each other. After that they sat down on the rocks to rest, their feet in the water.

Suddenly the sun went behind a cloud, and Broto looked up. The sun was getting low in the sky already. Had they been playing for so long? And the ducks! He jumped up.

"I must go, Amir," he said. "Pak Kasim will be back soon. Goodbye."

Broto quickly put his shirt on again and ran back to the bare rice field. Pak Kasim wasn't there yet, thank goodness. Now he wouldn't know how long Broto had been away.

But wait ... where were all the ducks? Some were still there, but what about the others?

Grabbing the bamboo pole, Broto ran off to look for them. He ran along the hard-baked edge of the rice field, and into the next field. No sign of the ducks. On he went, looking to right and left. Still no ducks. I'd better go back, he thought,

and look on the other side.

He passed the field where the ducks were. At last, beyond that field, he found the others. They were in a field of new rice plants, paddling in the water and trampling on the new green shoots. Oh dear! What on earth would the farmer say?

Broto herded the ducks together and led them back to their own field. Now to count and see if they were all there.

"Ninety eight, ninety nine ..." Broto counted again. No, he hadn't made a mistake. There was one missing! He would have to hurry and find it. He looked at the ducks. "Stay there," he said, "... please!"

Back Broto went to the fields he had searched before. He called and called, and waved his bamboo leaves. He hoped that perhaps the duck might see them. But there was no sign of that duck. He felt very miserable.

Broto was afraid to go any further, in case the other ducks wandered away again. Besides, the sun was getting low now and before long it would be dark.

Broto walked back to the field again and sat down. He thought about Pak Kasim. He had left his precious ducks with Broto, and now this had happened. Why had he left them alone to go swimming with Amir? Broto put his head in his hands, feeling ashamed.

Chapter 6

Pak Kasim comes back

Broto was so miserable that he didn't notice Pak Kasim walking towards him. Suddenly, there he was, holding a duck in his arms. Broto jumped up with joy at seeing the duck. Then put his head down again. No need to say anything. Pak Kasim knew.

"Where did you find it?" Broto asked.

"It was walking across the road," answered Pak Kasim.

On the road! Then Broto told Pak Kasim what had happened. How Amir had come and invited him for a swim. How he had played with Amir longer than he meant to. How some of the ducks had wandered off into the new rice field. And how he had searched for the missing duck, but couldn't find it. "I'm sorry, Pak Kasim," he said.

Pak Kasim listened quietly, though he frowned when he heard about the new rice shoots. Finally he said, "It's all right, Broto. I can see that you're sorry. And I'm glad I found the missing duck. Now it's getting late, and we must get you home before it's dark."

When they had brought the ducks together, and were walking along the road, Broto suddenly remembered Hanna. "What about Hanna?" he asked. "Did you find the doctor?"

"Yes," said Pak Kasim, "we took Hanna to the clinic, and the doctor gave her some medicine. Now she's not quite so hot, and she's sleeping."

Broto was glad. Something good had happened today, after all.

Chapter 7
Safely home

A fter a while, Pak Kasim said, "You were worried about the lost duck, weren't you?" Broto nodded.

"Do you know that God feels like that about us when we wander away from Him?"

"But we're not lost!" Broto objected.

"Well," said Pak Kasim slowly, "the Bible says we are. It says that when we do wrong things, and don't obey God, we're like the lost duck who wandered away. It tells a story about a boy who didn't want to obey his father any more. So he left his father's home, and did what he wanted, till all his money was gone, and still he wasn't happy."

"Then what did he do?" asked Broto.

"Then he suddenly realized how stupid he had been to leave his father who loved him. He decided to go back and say he was sorry."

"Did his father forgive him?"

Pak Kasim smiled. "He didn't just forgive him. He had been watching and waiting for his boy to come home. And he was so happy when he did come back that he had a big party to celebrate."

Broto could understand that. That was just how he felt when he saw the lost duck.

"So," finished Pak Kasim, "God is like that father. He is always waiting and longing for us to come back to Him. He made the way back through Jesus, who died for our sins."

They had left the road now and the ducks seemed to be walking a little faster as they came up the path to their pen. Pak Kasim opened the door of the duckpen and watched them all go through safely, one by one. Then he closed the door.

Broto looked up at Pak Kasim. "Can I talk to God now, and tell Him I'm sorry?"

Pak Kasim nodded. "You can talk to God anywhere, anytime, remember?"

Then, standing beside the duckpen, Broto prayed, "Dear God, I'm sorry for the wrong things I do. Please forgive me for Jesus' sake and make me like the boy that came home."

"Amen," said Pak Kasim, and he smiled at Broto's happy face. "Now, it's time we went home ... hey, why are you walking so fast?"

"Well," said Broto, "I want to tell my family how they can be found too!"

More OMF Books you will enjoy

IAN AND THE GIGANTIC LEAFY OBSTACLE, by Sheila Miller
"Teacher, why don't you pray now? Ask God to move the tree?"
  Ian was stuck, with a gigantic tree blocking his path down the mountain. And he did believe God answers prayer. But ... ask God to move a tree? Was it possible? What would happen if he did?

GRANNY HAN'S BREAKFAST, by Sheila Groves
It was time for breakfast—but there was no food in the house, and no money to buy any. Would Granny Han have to go hungry that day?
  Read this exciting true story to find out what happened.

MAKI'S BUSY WEEK, by Linda Hinchliffe
Maki's home is very different from yours, and the things he does are different too. In his busy week, Maki went to his mum's reading class, visited his friend Sami's baby brother, helped to do the washing in the river, and took his pig to church.

NEW TOES FOR TIA, by Larry Dinkins
Tia hated being different. She watched excitedly as the nurse took the bandages off her feet. Slowly she counted her pink toes. Would she now be like other children able to run barefoot, swim and explore adventurous places?
  Read this exciting story and find out.

WHEN PEOPLE PRAY *(Living Testimony Series)*

Denis Lane who has written the introduction to several of this series says in the introduction, "Prayer is a mystery — mysteries may frustrate us, but they are part of life — indeed the richest part of life." Is a person's experience of prayer the same in any country? Do answers come in the same way? Make up your own mind as you read the stories of 27 missionaries in many countries.

WHEN GOD GUIDES *(Living Testimony Series)*

Does God guide individuals? Is guidance confined to the big things of life, or must I refer everything to His direction? In this book guidance is clothed in flesh and blood! After Denis Lane's introductory chapter setting out ten principles for knowing God's guidance, 27 members of the OMF share their experiences in relation to marriage and children, houses and staff, missionary call and type of work, and the manifold details of everyday life.

WHEN GOD PROVIDES *(Living Testimony Series)*

Introductory chapter by Dr James H Taylor spells out the principles by which the OMF has lived for the past 120 years, and by which it still lives today. This is brought to life by over seventy testimonies covering topics which range from a second-hand tooth to a US$14,000 debt, from winter clothes in the right colours to the special need Asians have to give financial support to their parents. "The ultimate question is not what we do with our money but how deeply we trust in God."

WHEN THE ROOF CAVES IN *(Living Testimony Series)*
These testimonies tell of bereavement, accident, cot death, fire, sickness
and separation. Missionaries for whom the roof has also caved in bare
their hearts and share some of their feelings and experiences. Denis Lane
gives some pointers towards coping with such feelings, while veteran
Bible teacher J Oswald Sanders brings biblical insights on the whole
question of suffering.

TO A DIFFERENT DRUM, by Pauline G Hamilton
"Grabbing my sickle from the table, Mike began to run. I tore right after
him — I wasn't going to have him kill his father with my sickle!" Why
had Pauline Hamilton, a physiology Ph.D, chosen to march to a different
drum from her contemporaries, to experience danger and hardship in
China and Taiwan? Only because the God who saved her from suicide
and gave meaning to her life had called, and as she obeyed she found Him
faithful beyond all expectation.

GOLD FEARS NO FIRE, by Ralph Toliver
The panoramic story of the Lee family and their life in Communist
China.
 "A bullet zinged over the house. Another hit a tile on the roof and
shattered it. The fragments fell into the pig pen.
 "There was a rush of feet in the lane outside. Then a shout, rough, with
a northern accent. Then silence." It was 1949, and the Communists had
just arrived in the city of Chongqing, West China. For the Lee family,
life would never be the same again.